Mom,

Tell Me Why You're Catholic

and everything else you love

A Faith-Based Guided Journal to Celebrate a Mother's Joys

Sr. Gianna Casino, LIHM
Eileen Spinner, LPC

Catecases Press

THIS JOURNAL BELONGS TO

_____

_____

+ CATECASES +

Catecases Press: An imprint of Catecases, LLC
210 E. Main Street Unit 528, Jackson, MO 63755

ISBN-13: 979-8-9919702-0-4 (paperback)
IBSN-13: 979-8-9919702-1-1 (hardcover)
Library of Congress Control Number: 2024923910

"The loveliest masterpiece of the heart of God is the heart of a mother."

- St. Thérèse of Lisieux

CONTENTS

PREFACE

Welcome to "Mom, Tell Me Why You're Catholic, and Everything Else You Love." This journal is a heartfelt journey, designed to explore the stories, traditions, and values that shape your life. It's a space to connect what you love most with the people you love the most.

Take your time with each question. There's no right or wrong way to engage with the prompts; whether you choose to answer them in order or skip around, the important thing is to let your heart guide you. Some questions may resonate deeply, while others might not to you—and that's perfectly okay. Feel free to skip a question if you'd like and come up with more.

If writing feels too daunting some days, consider recording your voice. Sometimes, hearing the warmth of your voice or your loved one's voice can bring memories to life in ways words on a page cannot.

This journal is more than a collection of questions; it is an invitation to unfold your story—woven with faith, love, and the grace of God. As you reach the final pages, you'll discover a space for further reflection. Each moment you spend here is not just a gift to your loved ones, but a grace-filled offering to the One who writes the story of us all.

Dive in and discover the beautiful stories that shape our lives!

"I do not tremble when I see my weakness, for the treasures of a mother belong also to her child, and I am thy child, O dear Mother Mary."

- St. Therese of Liseaux

MOM'S ROOTS

"A people without the knowledge of their past history, origin, and culture is like a tree without roots." – Marcus Garvey

———— ❖ ————

What is your full name on your birth certificate?

_____

Birthdate:

_____ / _____ / _____

What city were you born in? What do you remember about your hometown?

_____

_____

_____

Where were your parents from?

_____

_____

Where were your grandparents from?

_____

_____

Share a story someone told you about your birth or about you as a baby.

_____

_____

_____

_____

_____

_____

What do you remember most about your family's spiritual or religious practices when you were young?

_____

_____

_____

_____

_____

"He gives the barren woman a home, making her the joyous mother of children. Praise the Lord!"

- Psalm 113:9

SACRAMENTS

The Eucharist is the source and summit of the Christian life."
– Catechism of the Catholic Church

———————— ✦ ————————

When and where were you baptized?

_____

What have others told you about your Baptism that is significant to you?

_____

_____

Describe your experience with Confession over the years. How has it changed from when you were a child until now?

_____

_____

_____

_____

_____

_____

_____

Tell me about your First Holy Communion.

_____

_____

_____

_____

What did you wear?

_____

How old were you?

_____

What do you remember about that day, receiving Jesus for the first time?

_____

_____

_____

What do you remember about your Confirmation?

_____

_____

How old were you?

_____

"Honor your father and your mother, that your days may be long in the land that the LORD your God is giving you."

- Exodus 20:12

GROWING UP

"Childhood is the soil in which the seeds of faith are planted."
– Unknown

———————◆———————

What memories come to mind when you think about going to Church with your family?

_____

_____

_____

_____

Who was the Pope when you were growing up? What do you remember about him?

_____

_____

_____

_____

How has the Catholic Church changed since you were young? How do you feel about these changes?

_____

_____

_____

How did your family celebrate Advent, Christmas and Epiphany when you were growing up?

_____

_____

How did your family celebrate Lent and Easter?

_____

_____

Name a saint or saints who particularly inspired you growing up... How did that saint or the saints influence your childhood?

_____

_____

_____

How would you describe your personality as a child? How did it change as you got older?

_____

_____

_____

_____

_____

What was a typical day like for you after school (e.g. sports, playing outside, dinner with family?)

_____

_____

_____

_____

_____

_____

_____

_____

_____

What were some of your favorite Christmas or birthday gifts? What made them so special?

_____

_____

_____

_____

_____

_____

_____

Did your family have pets? If so, did you have any favorites or favorite memories with them?

_____

_____

_____

_____

_____

_____

What types of things did you collect as a child, and what drew you to them? What things do you still collect?

_____

_____

_____

_____

_____

_____

What was your most prized possession when you were growing up? Where is it now?

_____

_____

_____

_____

Growing up, did you ever play an instrument, sing, or dance?

Instrument(s) _____

Singing _____

Dancing _____

What music did you listen to growing up and how did you listen to music?

_____

How have your musical interests changed throughout your life?

_____

What kinds of TV shows or movies did you watch as a child, if any?

_____

_____

Favorite book(s), magazine(s), or games as a child?

_____

_____

_____

_____

_____

"As one whom his mother comforts, so
I will comfort you."

- Isaiah 66:13

FAITH AND SPIRITUALITY

"Faith is to believe what you do not see; the reward of this faith is to see what you believe." – Saint Augustine

————————◆————————

What are your favorite prayers?

_____

_____

_____

_____

_____

_____

_____

_____

What are your favorite Church hymns or songs?

_____

_____

_____

_____

_____

_____

_____

_____

What is your favorite place to pray and meditate and why?

_____

What is your favorite liturgical season?

_____

In what ways do you see God every day?

_____

_____

_____

_____

_____

_____

What aspect of Catholic teachings do you find most beautiful or compelling? Why?

_____

_____

_____

_____

_____

_____

_____

_____

What aspect of Catholic teachings do you find most challenging or difficult? Why?

_____

_____

_____

_____

_____

_____

Who was the Pope during the most significant periods of your life, such as your youth, adulthood, or key moments in your faith journey?

_____

_____

_____

_____

How did his papacy influence your spiritual life during those times?

_____

_____

_____

_____

What are your favorite Bible verses or Book(s) of the Bible? (It's *okay if you need to look it up!*)

_____

_____

_____

_____

_____

_____

What is it about those Bible verses/Books of the Bible that is so meaningful to you?

_____

_____

_____

_____

Pick a favorite mystery of the rosary. What draws you to it?

_____

_____

_____

_____

How has Mary impacted your life? Share a memory of a time you really felt her presence.

_____

_____

_____

_____

_____

What statues, medals, or images of Mary have touched you the most?

_____

_____

_____

Who influenced your faith the most at different time periods of your life? And, how did they make an impact on you?

_____

_____

_____

_____

_____

_____

_____

_____

_____

"So now faith, hope, and love abide, these three; but the greatest of these is love."

- 1 Corinthians 13:13

GUARDIAN ANGELS AND SAINTS

"Our Guardian Angels are our most faithful friends, because they are with us day and night, always and everywhere. We ought often to invoke them." – St. John Vianney

———————◆———————

What do you believe about guardian angels?

_____

_____

_____

_____

_____

_____

_____

Share a time you may have felt or heard your guardian angel.

_____

_____

_____

_____

_____

_____

_____

Who are your favorite saints and why? How have they shown up throughout your life?

_____

_____

_____

_____

_____

What saint relics have you seen or touched?

_____

Do you or your family have any relics? If so, which ones?

_____

If you could have a relic of any saint, who would it be?

_____

Think of a special priest, religious sister, or religious brother—or maybe more than one—who had a significant impact on your life. How did each of them shape your spiritual journey?

_____

_____

_____

_____

_____

_____

"I can do all things through him who strengthens me."

- Philippians 4:13

FAITH IN ACTION

❅

When you think back on your life, what are some of the "God Wink" moments where you felt God intensely?

_____

_____

_____

_____

_____

_____

_____

_____

_____

_____

_____

_____

_____

_____

_____

_____

Describe a time when you saw God working through another person.

_____

_____

_____

_____

_____

_____

_____

_____

Have you ever witnessed or experienced a miracle? Numerous miracles?

_____

_____

_____

_____

_____

_____

_____

_____

_____

What are ways you've put your faith into action over the years?

_____

_____

_____

_____

_____

What was the hardest thing you had to give up for Lent?

_____

_____

_____

_____

Were you ever part of a youth group, faith sharing group, or Bible study group? Share some of the ones that really made an impact on you and others.

_____

_____

_____

_____

_____

_____

_____

_____

What role has the Eucharist played in your faith journey?

_____

_____

_____

_____

Share any special moments you had with the Eucharist.

_____

_____

_____

_____

Have you ever been on a pilgrimage?

_____

If so, where did you go and how did it impact you?

_____

_____

_____

_____

_____

_____

_____

"And Mary said: My soul glorifies the Lord and my spirit rejoices in God my Savior, for he has been mindful of the humble state of his servant. From now on all generations will call me blessed."

- Luke 1:46-48

PRAYER

"Prayer is the raising of one's mind and heart to God."
– Saint John Damascene

———————◆———————

What is your go-to prayer when you are troubled?

_____

_____

_____

_____

_____

Share about a time when prayer helped you through a difficult situation?

_____

_____

_____

_____

_____

_____

_____

_____

If you've been to Eucharistic Adoration, how do you pray? What do you do when you go to Adoration?

_____

_____

_____

_____

_____

_____

_____

List special devotions that are important to you.

_____

_____

_____

_____

_____

_____

What other religions or spiritual practices, if any, have taught you something or helped you grow into the person you are today?

_____

_____

_____

_____

_____

How do you know God is real?

_____

_____

_____

_____

_____

_____

_____

_____

_____

If you could ask God one question, what would it be?

_____

_____

_____

What novenas do you pray or have prayed in the past?

_____

_____

_____

_____

_____

_____

What have you struggled most with in your faith?

_____

_____

_____

_____

What's your vice?

_____

_____

What motivates you to embrace the Catholic faith? What excites you about it?

_____

_____

_____

_____

_____

"Her children rise up and call her blessed; Her husband also, and he praises her."

- Proverbs 31:2

FAVORITES AND FUN

"It's the little things in life that make the big picture beautiful."
– Unknown

———————◆———————

What are your favorite childhood memories?

_____

_____

_____

_____

_____

_____

_____

_____

What are your favorite quotes and why do they resonate with you?

_____

_____

_____

_____

_____

_____

_____

What is your favorite flower? Tree? Thing in nature?

_____

Did you have a favorite toy, stuffed animal friend, or doll?
What was its name?

_____

_____

Can you think of something that was special to you, but you
chose to give it to someone else? What made you decide to
give it away?

_____

_____

If you could be any animal for a day, which one would you
choose and why?

_____

If you could meet any fictional character from a book or movie,
who would it be?

_____

_____

If you could travel to any moment in time, what historical
event would you like to see and why?

_____

_____

What and who would you take on a deserted island?

_____

_____

_____

_____

_____

If someone gave you $1,000,000, and told you that you had twenty-four hours to give it all away to different people or charities, to whom would you give the money to?

_____

_____

_____

_____

_____

If you could have any person as a dinner party guest, who would it be and why?

_____

_____

_____

_____

If you could have any artist paint a portrait of you, who would you choose and why?

_____

What would you be doing in the painting?

_____

_____

Are there specific images, people or things in the painting with you?

_____

_____

List 4 things that comfort you.

1 _____

2 _____

3 _____

4 _____

List 4 things that bring you joy.

1 _____

2 _____

3 _____

4 _____

"Train up a child in the way he should go; even when he is old he will not depart from it."

- Proverbs 22:6

FAITH & FAMILY

"Family is the first school of Christian life and a school for human enrichment." – Pope St. John Paul II

———————◆———————

Tell me the story of how you and Dad met.

_____

_____

_____

_____

_____

_____

_____

What did you love most about Dad?

_____

_____

_____

What made you think he was the right man for you?

_____

_____

_____

_____

_____

_____

What do you remember most about your wedding day? (e.g. surprises, special moments, specific people, music, etc.)

_____

_____

_____

_____

_____

How did the sacrament of marriage strengthen your relationship with Dad?

_____

_____

_____

_____

_____

Who or what was most helpful to you and Dad during difficult times?

_____

_____

_____

_____

_____

List 3 things you love most about each of your children.

1 _____
2 _____
3 _____

1 _____
2 _____
3 _____

1 _____
2 _____
3 _____

1 _____
2 _____
3 _____

What qualities or characteristics of yours or Dad's do you see in your children?

_____
_____
_____
_____
_____
_____

"Look at the mothers who truly love their children: how many sacrifices they make for them. They are ready for everything, even to give their own blood so that their babies grow up good, healthy, and strong."

- St. Gianna Beretta Molla

MOTHERHOOD

"Motherhood: All love begins and ends there."
– Robert Browning

———————◆———————

What challenges or surprises (if any) did you face during your pregnancy and postpartum with your children?

_____
_____
_____

Describe how it felt when you became a mother.

_____
_____
_____
_____
_____

What did you sing to me when I was a baby?

_____
_____

What music did you play for me?

_____
_____

(For a grandmother) Describe how it felt to become a grandmother and see your child as a parent?

_____

_____

_____

_____

_____

What was the hardest part about being a parent for you?

_____

_____

_____

_____

_____

_____

How did your faith influence you or help you as a mother?

_____

_____

_____

_____

_____

If you could change one thing about how you raised me, what would it be?

_____

_____

_____

_____

Share with me a time you were worried you made the wrong decision as a parent.

_____

_____

_____

_____

What do you think was the most important lesson you tried to teach me growing up?

_____

_____

_____

Looking back, what are you most proud of in how you raised me?

_____

_____

_____

_____

What is something about me that surprised you as I grew up?

_____

_____

_____

_____

What are some favorite memories you have of your own parents with your children? How did your parents directly or indirectly impact your children?

_____

_____

_____

_____

_____

_____

_____

Share with me a moment from my childhood that you wish you could go back to and experience again.

_____

_____

_____

_____

_____

How did being a parent change you over the years?

_____

_____

_____

_____

What's your greatest parenting advice to others?

_____

_____

_____

_____

What is a secret that you always kept from your own mother?

_____

_____

_____

_____

What is a secret that you always kept from me?

_____

_____

_____

_____

"For where you go I will go, and where you lodge I will lodge. Your people shall be my people, and your God my God."

- Ruth 1:16-17

LITERATURE/FILM/MUSIC

"Art, whether it's music, painting, or literature, is how we express the soul's deepest emotions." – Unknown

———◆———

What is one book that has had a profound impact on your life?

_____

_____

_____

_____

_____

_____

_____

Think about a movie or specific movie scene that resonates with you. What captures your attention?

_____

_____

_____

_____

_____

_____

_____

_____

If your life was a novel, what would the title be?

_____

_____

If your life were made into a feature film, which actress would you choose to play you?

_____

Who are your favorite author(s) or inspirational speaker(s)? What do you love about them?

_____

_____

_____

What are your favorite songs to sing or listen to and why?

_____

_____

_____

_____

"A married woman must, when called upon, leave her devotions to God at the altar to find Him in her household affairs."

—St. Frances of Rome

FOOD/RECIPES

❖

When you look back on your life, who were your favorite cooks or bakers? What did they make that was so special?

_____

_____

_____

What food could you not live without?

_____

What is your favorite thing to cook or bake?

_____

What is the strangest food you have ever tasted?

_____

What is the greatest food you have ever tasted?

_____

What are your favorite fancy and fast food places to eat?

_____

If you could have one more meal, what would it be?

_____

"That special power of loving that belongs to a woman is seen most clearly when she becomes a mother. Motherhood is the gift of God to women. How grateful we must be to God for this wonderful gift that brings such joy to the whole world, women and men alike!"

- St. Teresa of Calcutta

SPORTS

"The strength of the team is each individual member. The strength of each member is the team." – Phil Jackson

———————— ✤ ————————

What sport(s) did you play growing up?

_____

What sport(s) did you excel at and enjoy the most?

_____

_____

What's your favorite sport to watch?

_____

If you could be a pro at a sport, what would it be?

_____

What are your favorite sports teams?

_____

_____

What are your favorite memories of your children in sports?

_____

_____

_____

_____

"Whatever is true, whatever is noble, whatever is right, whatever is pure, whatever is lovely, whatever is admirable-if anything is excellent or praiseworthy-think about such things."

- Philippians 4:8

WOULD YOU PREFER

Would you prefer

- A Pilgrimage **or** a Silent Retreat

- The Traditional Latin Mass **or** The Norvus Ordo Mass (Ordinary Form)

- A quiet evening at home **or** a lively night out with friends

- Indoors **or** Outdoors

- Coffee **or** Tea

- Home-cooked meals **or** Takeout

- Early mornings **or** Late nights

- A Safari **or** a Cruise

- Routine **or** Spontaneity

- Dogs **or** Cats

or Both, and Why?

_____   _____

_____   _____

_____   _____

_____   _____

_____   _____

"Near the cross of Jesus stood his mother. When Jesus saw his mother there, and the disciple whom he loved standing nearby, he said to his mother, 'Dear woman, here is your son,' and to the disciple, 'Here is your mother.' From that time on, this disciple took her into his home."

- John 19:25-27

WOULD YOU RATHER

"So whether you eat or drink, or whatever you do,
do it all for the glory of God." – 1 Corinthians 10:31

Would you rather

- Preach like St. Peter **or** Write like St. Paul

- Read a book **or** Listen to a podcast/radio

- Retire **or** Work actively

- Cook **or** Bake

- Garden **or** Clean

- Go to the beach **or** Go to the mountains

- Swim in a pool **or** Swim in the ocean

or Both, and Why?

_____

_____

_____

_____

_____

_____

"The most important person on earth is a mother. She cannot claim the honor of having built Notre Dame Cathedral. She need not. She has built something more magnificent than any cathedral — a dwelling for an immortal soul, the tiny perfection of her baby's body. ... The angels have not been blessed with such a grace. They cannot share in God's creative miracle to bring new saints to heaven. Only a human mother can."

-Cardinal József Mindszenty

TRAVEL AND ADVENTURES

"The world is a book, and those who do not travel read only one page."
-St. Augustine

Mark the places you have traveled to on the map below.

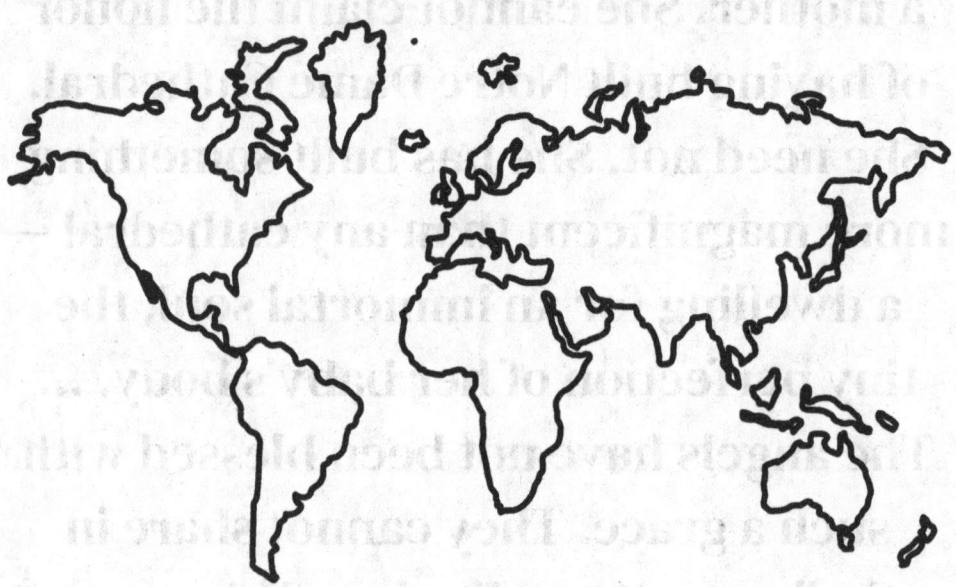

Share about your 3 favorite places.

1 _____

2 _____

3 _____

What is the most adventurous thing you did on your travels?

_____

"Thank you, women who are mothers...
This experience makes you become
God's own smile upon the newborn
child, the one who guides your child's
first steps, who helps it to grow, and
who is the anchor as the child makes its
way along the journey of life."

- Pope St. John Paul II

PEARLS OF WISDOM

"Wisdom is not a product of schooling but of the lifelong attempt to acquire it." – Albert Einstein

———————— ❖ ————————

What's the most valuable lesson about faith you hope to pass on to me?

_____

_____

_____

_____

How have you tried to model faith for our family?

_____

_____

_____

Do you believe "everything happens for a reason"? Why or why not?

_____

_____

_____

_____

Name 4 things you're glad you learned in school.

1 _____

2 _____

3 _____

4 _____

What did you love most about your job? (If you spent time at home, what did you love most about that?)

_____

_____

_____

_____

What were some of the most meaningful things you did in terms of volunteer work for the community, church or my school?

_____

_____

_____

_____

Tell me about a time you thought something wouldn't work out, but it did.

_____

_____

_____

How do you bounce back and rise from difficult situations?

_____

_____

_____

_____

_____

How do you establish healthy boundaries with people in your life?

_____

_____

_____

_____

_____

_____

How would you describe a true friend? Tell me about some of your truest friends.

_____

_____

_____

_____

_____

_____

What's the most challenging thing you've ever accomplished?

_____

_____

_____

What is one piece of advice you would give to your younger self?

_____

_____

_____

_____

What is one thing you would like to change about the world and why?

_____

_____

_____

_____

What is your favorite way to inspire or motivate others?

_____

_____

_____

_____

_____

If you had the chance to thank someone from your past, who would it be and why?

_____

_____

_____

_____

Name 5 things you are grateful for.

1 _____

2 _____

3 _____

4 _____

5 _____

Name 10 people you are grateful for.

1 _____

2 _____

3 _____

4 _____

5 _____

6 _____

7 _____

8 _____

9 _____

10 _____

Circle the values that mean the most to you (and add others that might not be listed here.)

ACCOUNTABILITY	FAMILY	PATIENCE
ACHIEVEMENT	FLEXIBILITY	PEACE
ADAPTABILITY	FREEDOM	POWER
APPRECIATION	FRIENDSHIP	PRODUCTIVITY
AUTONOMY	GENEROSITY	PROSPERITY
BALANCE	GROWTH	QUALITY
BEAUTY	HAPPINESS	RECOGNITION
CHALLENGE	HARMONY	RESPECT
COMMUNICATION	HEALTH	RELATIONSHIPS
CONNECTION	HONESTY	SECURITY
COURAGE	HOPE	SERVICE
CREATIVITY	HUMOR	SIMPLICITY
CURIOSITY	INDEPENDENCE	SPIRITUALITY
DEPENDABILITY	INTEGRITY	STABILITY
DISCIPLINE	INTELLIGENCE	STRENGTH
DIVERSITY	JOY	TEAMWORK
EDUCATION	JUSTICE	TRANQUILITY
EFFECTIVENESS	LOVE/AFFECTION	TRUST
EMPATHY	LOYALTY	TRUTH
FAITH	OPENNESS	WISDOM

Write your top 5 values below.

1 _____

2 _____

3 _____

4 _____

5 _____

What is a great compliment you remember receiving?

_____

_____

_____

_____

_____

What are some things your parents taught you that you're especially grateful for?

_____

_____

_____

_____

_____

What is some advice or words of wisdom others taught you that influenced the way you lived your life?

_____

_____

_____

_____

_____

What is some advice or words of wisdom you want to give to me?

_____

_____

_____

_____

What would you want your legacy to be?

_____

_____

_____

How do you want to be remembered?

_____

_____

_____

_____

_____

_____

_____

_____

"Do not be troubled or weighed down with grief. Do not fear any illness or vexation, anxiety or pain. Am I not here who am your Mother? Are you not under my shadow and protection? Am I not your fountain of life? Are you not in the folds of my mantle? In the crossing of my arms? Is there anything else you need?"

- Our Lady of Guadalupe to St. Juan Diego

DEDICATION

To: Rubilinda Gimena Casino

Mama,

You will always be my world and the strongest person I know.
You've taught me everything I know about being a mother.
I look forward to the day when I see you and Dad again in
Heaven. We are forever in the arms of Mary. I'll always see her
love in yours.

Your Madre Anak,
Sister Gianna

To: Mary Therese Rakowitz

Mamacita,

I am so blessed to be your daughter. Your humility, generosity,
and deep faith have always inspired me, and I know my life is
abundantly blessed because of your prayers. Thank you for
helping me become the woman I am today with a strong faith
and deep compassion for others.

I love you!
Eileen "Daughter Dearest"

ENDNOTE

As you fill this journal, may the love, faith, and wisdom you've explored here continue to guide you and inspire those around you. These pages hold not just questions, but invitations to dive deeper into the stories that make up your beautiful life. It's not about finding all the answers but cherishing the journey and the conversations that arise along the way.

Keep your heart open to the little blessings that come your way—they're reminders of the love that surrounds us all.

ROOM FOR MORE

www.ingramcontent.com/pod-product-compliance
Lightning Source LLC
Chambersburg PA
CBHW011239120626
46549CB00009B/3341